EDWOOD COAST

NATURAL WONDERS

Jason Cooper

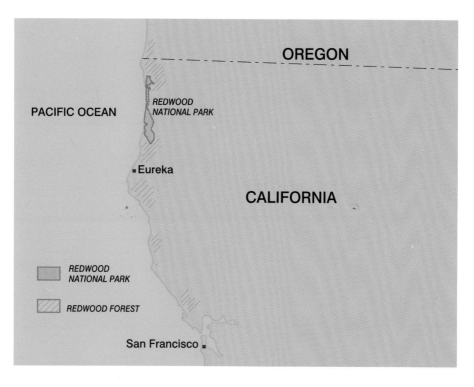

The Rourke Press, Inc.
Vero Beach, Florida 32964

PHOTO CREDITS
All photos © Lynn N. Stone except page 15 © James P. Rowan

Library of Congress Cataloging-in-Publication Data

Cooper, Jason, 1942-
    The Redwood Coast / Jason Cooper
       p. cm. — (Natural Wonders)
    Includes index.
    ISBN 1-57103-018-2
    1. Redwood National Park (Calif.)—Juvenile literature.
2. Redwood—Juvenile literature. [1. Redwood National Park
(Calif.) 2. National parks and reserves 3. Redwood.]
I. Title II. Series: Cooper, Jason, 1942-   Natural Wonders.
F868.R4C66 1995
979.4' 12—dc20   95–12307
                                                              CIP
                                                              AC

Printed in the USA

TABLE OF CONTENTS

THE REDWOOD COAST

America's Far West has an amazing forest of living giants. This is the forest of towering redwood trees. It hugs the Pacific coast for about 450 miles, from central California north into southern Oregon.

Redwoods grow only within 30 miles of the Pacific Ocean. Winter rain and summer fog keep the forest giants moist and healthy.

Redwoods are remarkable trees. They are the world's tallest trees and some of the oldest.

A forest like no other, the redwoods hug the Pacific coast of central and northern California

THE GIANT REDWOODS

An average adult redwood stands about 240 feet. That's almost the length of a football field. The **sequoia** (seh KWOI uh) tree, a close relative, is thicker but shorter. The tallest redwoods rise 360 feet, higher than the Statue of Liberty!

California's oldest redwoods have passed their 2000th birthday. They were alive during the time of Christ and long before Christopher Columbus.

Redwoods resist disease, insects, storms, and fire. About their only enemy is the logger's saw.

Tallest of the long-lived redwoods reach over 300 feet—and disappear in hanging clouds

LIFE IN THE REDWOODS

Redwood forests are a community of plants and animals. Redwood trees often live among other big trees, such as western hemlock and Douglas fir.

The great trees keep the forest dark and cool. Without much sunlight, fairly few plants survive beneath the redwoods. Each spring, however, the blossoms of **rhododendron** (ro do DEN drun) shrubs and wildflower blooms brighten the dim forest floor.

Redwoods like the low, moist coastal country. They thin out as the ground rises east of the coast.

Rhododendron blooms brighten a grove in Redwood National Park

ANIMALS

The animals of the forest live quietly in the deep shadows. Now and then a bird's song or a squirrel's scratching disturbs the stillness.

Roosevelt elk are the biggest animals of the redwoods. They feed in open grassy areas, then retreat to the forest to rest and hide. Black bears, skunks, spotted owls, and slimy **slugs** (SLUHGZ) also live in the redwoods.

Antlers in summer velvet, a Roosevelt elk munches grass in Prairie Creek Redwood State Park

Perhaps the slimiest members of the redwood community, banana slugs crawl on the bark of a redwood

A trail in Redwood National Park leads to this green scene in Fern Canyon

PEOPLE IN THE REDWOODS

Native Americans may have lived along the Redwood coast as long as 10,000 years ago. A Spanish explorer, Juan Rodriguez Cabrillo, probably sailed along the redwood coast in 1542. The first person to bring the redwoods to world attention, however, was another Spaniard, Don Gaspar de Portola, in 1769.

In the 1800's, American pioneers flocked to California. Some viewed the ancient redwood forests as too amazing to cut. Others felt the forests were too valuable *not* to cut.

Tiny in a forest of giants, a visitor explores a redwood grove

BATTLES OVER THE FOREST

The hard, reddish wood of redwoods is very valuable lumber. Like the living trees, redwood lumber is tough. Timber companies love it for building and other wood products.

Timber companies began cutting redwoods in the 1820's. Ever since, people have argued about whether to keep or cut redwoods. They've done some of both.

Redwoods once covered about 2,000,000 acres. Three-quarters of that area has either been cut over or is owned by timber companies.

America's appetite for redwood products has put a mighty dent in the old growth redwood forests

THE STATE PARKS

California first acted to protect a small forest of redwoods in 1902. With the help of the Save-the-Redwoods League, the state has continued to add redwood parks.

Today California has 180,000 acres of redwood forest in 36 state parks. About one-third of the state-owned forests have never been cut. These are the **ancient** (AIN chent), or **old-growth** (OLD-groth) forests, the forests with the oldest and tallest trees.

California's 36 state parks with redwood forests protect thousands of old-growth acres

REDWOOD NATIONAL PARK

The U.S. Government first helped to protect old redwood forests in 1907. It created Muir Woods National Monument, a small redwood preserve near San Francisco.

In 1968, the U.S. Government created Redwood National Park on the northern California coast. The park includes 20,000 acres of old-growth forests. It also protects about 60,000 acres of seacoast and "new" redwood forest. This new forest is growing up again after having been cut.

Redwood Creek slips past the forest of giants in Redwood National Park

VISITING THE REDWOODS

Like narrow valleys, highways lead through the deep redwood forests. The best way to "feel" a redwood forest, though, is to hike in it.

Hikers like the silent redwood forest when spears of sunlight pierce the morning fogs. A favorite hiker's path follows Redwood Creek in the national park. Another park trail winds into a cool, dark canyon whose walls are feathered with ferns.

Glossary

ancient (AIN chent) — very old

old-growth (OLD groth) — forest that has never been logged; a forest in its original condition

rhododendron (ro do DEN drun) — any of several related shrubs with bright flowers and leathery evergreen leaves

sequoia (seh KWOI uh) — a tall, thick tree of California's Sierra Nevada Mountains; a shorter, thicker cousin of the coast redwood tree

slug (SLUHG) — a snail without a shell; one of the soft, boneless animals in the mollusk group

INDEX